WITHDRAWN

D1292036

Crocodiles

ABDO
Publishing Company

A Buddy Book
by
Julie Murray

VISIT US AT
www.abdopub.com

Published by Buddy Books, an imprint of ABDO Publishing Company, 4940 Viking Drive, Suite 622, Edina, Minnesota 55435. Copyright © 2005 by Abdo Consulting Group, Inc. International copyrights reserved in all countries. No part of this book may be reproduced in any form without written permission from the publisher.

Printed in the United States.

Edited by: Christy DeVillier
Contributing Editors: Matt Ray, Michael P. Goecke
Graphic Design: Maria Hosley
Image Research: Deborah Coldiron
Photographs: Corbis, corel, Minden Pictures

Library of Congress Cataloging-in-Publication Data

Murray, Julie, 1969-
   Crocodiles/Julie Murray.
      p. cm. — (Animal kingdom. Set II)
   Contents: Reptiles — Crocodiles — What they look like — Where they live — What they eat — Senses — Defenses — Babies — Crocodile or alligator?
   ISBN 1-59197-311-2
      1. Crocodiles—Juvenile literature. [1. Crocodiles] I. Title.

QL666.C925 M873 2003
597.98'2—dc21

                                                    2002037915

Contents

Crocodiles Are Reptiles

Crocodiles have been around for millions of years. They were even here when dinosaurs walked the earth. Like the dinosaurs, crocodiles are reptiles. Alligators, lizards, snakes, and turtles are reptiles, too.

Reptiles are ectothermic animals. Ectothermic animals cannot make heat inside their bodies. Reptiles must lie in sunshine to get warm. They need shade or water to cool down.

Lying in sunshine helps crocodiles warm up.

Crocodiles And Alligators

Crocodiles and alligators are related. They belong to a group called crocodilians.

Crocodiles and alligators look alike. One way to tell these crocodilians apart is to look at their snouts. An alligator's snout is shorter and wider than a crocodile's. It is rounded at the end. When an alligator's mouth is closed, its lower teeth are hidden.

A crocodile has a longer snout. It is more pointed on the end. Some of a crocodile's lower teeth show when its mouth is closed.

Alligator

Crocodile

What They Look Like

There are 14 kinds of crocodiles. Like other reptiles, they have tough skin with scales. A crocodile's skin may be brown, black, green, tan, or gray.

Crocodiles are the largest reptiles around today.

Most crocodiles grow to become about 11 feet (3 m) long. Indo-Pacific crocodiles can grow more than 20 feet (6 m) long. African dwarf crocodiles are smaller. They only grow about five feet (two m) long.

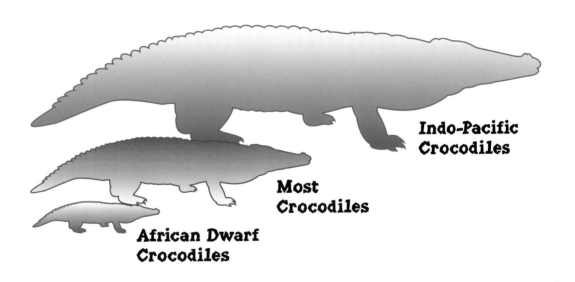

Indo-Pacific Crocodiles

Most Crocodiles

African Dwarf Crocodiles

20 feet (6 meters)

A crocodile's eyes, ears, and nose are on the top of its head. So, these reptiles can see, hear, and smell while floating in water.

A crocodile has four short legs. It has a long tail for swimming. Crocodiles can swim as fast as nine miles (15 km) per hour. They can walk on land, too.

Crocodiles can see, hear, and smell while floating in water.

Where They Live

Crocodiles live in tropical areas around the world. The American crocodile lives in Florida, Mexico, Central America, and northern South America. The Nile crocodile lives in Africa. The Indo-Pacific crocodile lives in India, Southeast Asia, New Guinea, the Philippines, and northern Australia.

Crocodiles spend much of their time in water. They live near swamps, rivers, and lakes. The Indo-Pacific crocodile can live in salt water. Many people call it the saltwater crocodile.

Crocodiles live near water.

Hunting And Eating

Crocodiles are predators. They hunt and eat animals. Crocodiles eat frogs, fish, and birds. Large crocodiles may eat larger animals, such as deer or zebras.

This Nile crocodile is eating a baboon.

Crocodiles often ambush their prey. This means they take animals by surprise. Crocodiles hide quietly waiting for prey. When an animal comes close, they grab it quickly.

Crocodiles may ambush prey by lying quietly in water.

Crocodiles have strong jaws for biting. But they do not chew their food. Crocodiles swallow small animals whole. They rip apart big animals before eating them.

Crocodiles can live for a long time without eating. Small ones can live four months without eating. Large crocodiles can live for a year without food.

Crocodile Teeth

People only grow two sets of teeth. But crocodiles never stop growing new teeth. When a crocodile's tooth falls out, a new tooth grows in its place. An adult crocodile may have about 60 teeth at one time. It may use hundreds of teeth in its lifetime.

Guarding Against Enemies

Crocodiles can protect themselves well against enemies. Bony plates under their skin helps shield them from animal bites. Crocodiles can run or swim away from danger, too.

Adult crocodiles are safe from most animals.

Crocodiles can fight enemies by biting. Crocodiles fight with their strong tails, too. A crocodile can knock down a large animal with its tail.

Crocodiles are good fighters.

Baby Crocodiles

Crocodiles lay their eggs in nests. Some mother crocodiles build nests with mud and plants. Others dig a hole in the sand.

Female crocodiles lay between 15 and 90 eggs at one time. They cover their eggs with sand, mud, or leaves. This keeps the eggs warm and hides them from egg-eating animals.

Crocodile eggs hatch after about three months. A newborn crocodile is less than 12 inches (30 cm) long. It weighs about three ounces (85 g). The mother crocodile carries her babies to the water. She watches over them for a few months. Baby crocodiles must watch out for fish, lizards, snakes, and birds. These animals eat baby crocodiles.

A baby crocodile hatching.

Crocodiles can live long lives. Nile crocodiles can live as long as 70 years. Some crocodiles have lived for 100 years.

Crocodiles are amazing reptiles.

Important Words

ambush hiding in order to surprise something or someone.

ectothermic describes animals that cannot make heat inside their bodies.

predator an animal that hunts and eats other animals.

prey an animal that is food for another animal.

reptiles ectothermic animals with lungs, scales, and a backbone.

scales flat plates that form the outer covering of reptiles.

tropical weather that is warm and wet.

Web Sites

To learn more about crocodiles, visit ABDO Publishing Company on the World Wide Web. Web sites about crocodiles are featured on our Book Links page. These links are routinely monitored and updated to provide the most current information available.

www.abdopub.com

Index